Everything You Need to Know About

DEALING WITH
THE POLICE

Many police officers are just doing their job. Others, however, step beyond the bounds of the law.

• THE NEED TO KNOW LIBRARY •

Everything You Need to Know About

DEALING WITH THE POLICE

Maryann Miller

THE ROSEN PUBLISHING GROUP, INC.
NEW YORK

Published in 1995 by The Rosen Publishing Group, Inc.
29 East 21st Street, New York, NY 10010

First Edition

Manufactured in the United States of America

Library of Congress Cataloging-in-Publication Data

Miller, Maryann, 1943–
    Everything you need to know about dealing with the police /
Maryann Miller. — 1st ed.
        p.   cm. — (The need to know library)
    Includes bibliographical references and index.
    ISBN 0-8239-1875-0
    1. Police—Juvenile literature.   2. Assistance in emergencies—
Juvenile literature.   [1. Police.   2. Assistance in emergencies.]
I. Title.   II. Series.
HV7922.M5   1994
363.2—dc20   94-18526
                                                                     CIP
                                                                      AC

Contents

Introduction

*G*reg was spending the night with his buddy, John. Then they got into a stupid argument, and Greg decided to go home. He stormed out to his car and got in before he realized it was one o'clock in the morning. He couldn't go home. Dad had told him never to drive after eleven o'clock.

After driving around for a while, Greg stopped in a quiet neighborhood. He'd just sleep in the car. No big deal. Then he could go home in the morning.

About an hour later, a loud banging woke Greg up. A bright light glared through the window. A loud, gruff voice said, "Out of the car! Now!"

The light moved just enough for Greg to see a police officer standing there. What on earth was wrong? Was it illegal to sleep in your own car?

Greg opened the door and started to get out. Rough hands grabbed him and pushed him to the ground. Greg tried to protest, tried to ask why this was happening. He was rudely told to keep his mouth shut and put his hands behind his back. Handcuffs clicked into place, and Greg was ordered not to move. Numb with fear, he obeyed.

Sometimes we find ourselves in the wrong place at the wrong time.

Suddenly another patrol car pulled up, and two officers and a civilian man walked over. The civilian looked at Greg. "No, that's not the guy."

Then he looked at Greg's car. "That's not the car, either."

Now Greg at least had a clue to what was happening: He'd been mistaken for someone else.

The police officer unlocked the handcuffs and told Greg to get up. Expecting an explanation and perhaps even an apology, Greg was stunned when the officer turned on him. He gruffly told Greg to get in his car and go home. The tirade ended with a warning that if he ever caught Greg out at two in the morning again, it wouldn't go so easy.

That incident occurred in a suburb of Dallas. Do you think Greg had a bad feeling about police officers after that? Do you blame him?

Not everyone has such a frightening first encounter with police officers. Most of the time it's just an embarrassing ticket for a traffic violation.

And to be fair, not all police officers act like the one Greg met. Our problem as citizens is that we don't know which officer we are going to meet.

Looking at it from the other side for a moment, we have to realize that the officers don't know whom they are encountering either.

In Greg's situation, the officers did act appropriately up to a point. They were responding

Chances are likely that your encounters with the police are on a friendly or helpful basis.

to a call about a young, white male burglar who had fled the scene in a red car.

Greg was in a red car a few blocks from where the crime had occurred. The officer had no choice but to consider that he might be the burglar. The officer's job was to catch the criminal and ask questions later.

The officer stepped out of bounds by being unnecessarily rough. He also could have questioned Greg. Not that he should have just taken Greg's word. But if the officer had learned enough to suspect he had the wrong guy, he might have treated Greg differently.

Greg also deserved an apology, not a threat.

The officer could have talked to Greg about the dangers of being out alone so late. Greg certainly would have left the scene with a better attitude about the police.

Instead, Greg left angry and resentful.

With luck, your first encounter with the police won't be so frightening. But chances are you will have contact with the police at one time or another.

In this book we look at some situations you might face and also at ways you can avoid difficulties with the police. Reading it will tell you what the police can and cannot do and what your rights are in certain situations.

The United States Coast Guard is one of the several federal law-enforcement agencies.

Chapter 1

Just a Few Facts

Before we get into specific situations, let's see how law enforcement operates.

The United States has three levels of law enforcement, the federal, state, and local. The agencies on the federal level are the Federal Bureau of Investigation (FBI); the Drug Enforcement Administration (DEA); the Immigration Border Patrol; the U.S. Customs Service; the U.S. Secret Service; the Bureau of Alcohol, Tobacco, and Firearms; the Postal Inspection Service; and the U.S. Coast Guard.

State agencies are called variously the State Police, Highway Patrol, or State Patrol.

The two main agencies at the local level are the municipal police department and the county sheriff's department. The police departments serve in towns and cities. The sheriff's department covers areas outside town or city limits. Sometimes both agencies serve in the same area, in which case the sheriff's department is responsible for operating the jail.

The city police department is the agency we are most likely to have contact with. The patrol officers are the ones who stop us for traffic violations. They respond to emergency calls and reports of crime. They go to accident scenes to offer assistance and take reports.

In Canada, the Royal Canadian Mounted Police enforce federal laws throughout the country and perform the function of provincial police in all provinces except Ontario and Quebec.

On the Streets

Each patrol officer covers a section of the city that is called his *beat*. He is responsible for the protection of the homes and businesses on his beat. Most of his time is spent either driving or walking his beat.

The patrol officer also responds to reports of crime relayed to him by the dispatcher. The dispatcher can also send him to another area as a backup for other officers.

When officers respond to a report, they must be prepared for any possibility. Under *Condition Red*, officers would go in with their weapons drawn. A known threat, such as gunshots being fired, would indicate Condition Red.

For a less specific threat, officers use Condition

Yellow. A report of a prowler would represent a possibility of danger or violence. The officers would be prepared, while doing everything possible to prevent violence.

When making an arrest or controlling a situation, officers may use several steps of force:

Verbal—Telling the person he is under arrest and what the charge is. If the person surrenders quietly, no further steps are taken.

Physical contact—If a person tries to run, the officers can seize him to make the arrest.

Mace—Can be used to control a person who poses an immediate threat or danger.

Nightstick—Can be used to subdue a person who is fighting. (People who are high on drugs often resist with amazing strength.)

Gun—Called *deadly force,* use of a gun is authorized against an immediate violent threat.

Part of an officer's training is learning when and how to use each step of force. Good reason is required to move beyond the first step.

Officers may not draw their weapon on an unarmed suspect, but the threat does not have to be a gun. It could be a club, a knife, or even a screwdriver used in a threatening manner.

Chapter 2

The Traffic Ticket

*I*t was late when Jenny left. She had only ten minutes to pick up Marcy and get to dance class by seven o'clock. Did she dare speed?

Yeah, just this once. She hardly ever saw cops along this stretch of road. It would be all right.

Jenny stepped on it.

A block from Marcy's, Jenny heard the siren. No, please God, don't let it be.

Jenny looked in her rear-view mirror and saw the flashing lights. "Oh, man," she said. "My folks are going to kill me!"

Being pulled over is something we all dread. It's embarrassing. Everyone driving by is going to know we did something foolish. Besides, we were already late, and now we're going to be even later. We'll have to deal with the ticket *and* our parents.

We all have to accept the consequences of

Always have your driver's license, the car's registration papers, and the insurance information on hand when you are driving.

breaking the law. But how we act and react to the officer who stops us can make the experience a little less painful.

Joey

When Joey was stopped for speeding, he was angry. "Hey, that other guy was speeding, too," he said. "Why didn't you stop him?"

The comment irritated the officer, who didn't want to be told how to do his job and didn't like Joey's belligerent attitude.

It didn't help that Joey couldn't find his car

registration and insurance card. He did have his driver's license, but that wasn't enough. He should have had all the required information.

Joey got a ticket.

Always be sure you have your license, registration, and insurance card with you when you drive.

Most people keep their registration and proof of insurance in the glove compartment of the car. If the papers are not in the car you drive, ask your parents where they are. Then put them in the car yourself.

What to Do When You're Stopped

People used to think they should get out of the car when stopped by a police officer. That isn't true. If the officer does not know why you are getting out, he or she could feel threatened. Many police officers have been killed by people they stop for routine traffic violations.

Stay in your car. Roll down your window and keep your hands on the steering wheel. Wait for the officer to ask for your license and registration. Don't just reach for the glove compartment. Tell the officer you are getting the papers. That way he or she doesn't have to guess. If you just make a sudden move, the officer might again feel threatened and react.

Keep your hands on the steering wheel if pulled over by the police.

"That's silly," you may be thinking. "Why should an officer feel threatened by me? I'm not going to do anything."

The point is, *you* know that. The officer doesn't.

Just for a moment, put yourself in the officer's position. He stops a lot of people for routine traffic violations. Most of them are average citizens who present no danger. But some of them are criminals who will do anything to keep from going back to jail. They won't hesitate to use a gun.

Be polite, and don't pretend you don't know what you did wrong. One officer says he doesn't like to be asked. "Most people know what they did," he says. "Trying to play innocent won't impress most officers. We're tired of hearing it."

However, if you honestly don't know what you did wrong, you can say so. For example, Dave was driving in an unfamiliar part of town and didn't know that the speed limit changed from 40 to 30 miles per hour. When Dave explained that, the officer didn't give him a ticket; Dave got off with a warning to watch the speed-limit signs.

Dave was lucky. Officers seldom accept excuses, even from adults. But if you are polite and sincere, you increase your chances of being lucky.

One officer admits that he is harder on teen drivers than adults. "It may not seem fair," he says. "But I've just been at too many accidents where teens have died. If I give a kid a ticket and he thinks twice about speeding the next time, I might save his life. It's that simple."

Paying the Consequences

If you do receive a ticket, you will have to pay a fine. The amount of the fine varies, depending on the violation. Fines for speeding are based on how much the driver was exceeding the speed limit at the time.

When you receive a traffic ticket, you are given a date to appear in Municipal Court. That is where all nonfelony cases are heard. You and the officer who gave you the ticket appear on the scheduled day. Each of you tells your side of the incident, and the judge decides whether you are guilty or not. If you are found guilty, you then pay the fine.

You don't have to go to court, however. If you agree that you deserved the ticket, you can just pay the fine. The ticket contains information on how to do so before your court date. When you pay the fine, the offense then becomes part of your record.

If you want to take care of the ticket without having a permanent record, there may be a way. If your city has a Teen Court, you can appear there for a hearing. Teen Courts are run entirely by teens, with an adult judge. A teen jury hears your case and then sentences you to a time of community service. When you have served those hours, your record is wiped clean as if the offense never occurred.

At least fourteen states now have Teen Courts. You can find out if there is one in your city by calling the Municipal Court. The number is in the phone book under the listings for city services. Teen Courts try only Class C misdemeanors. Those are crimes that are not serious: traffic violations, truancy, curfew violations, disrupting a classroom, and simple assault.

Many teens have taken the option of going to Teen Court and are glad they did.

Chapter 3

In Your Face

"*I* have to go check on the house that we rent out," Stacy said. "You guys want to come with me?"

Her friends agreed. After they looked over the house, they'd go hang out at the arcade for a while.

At the house, Stacy told her friends to wait in the living room while she inspected the paint job in the back rooms. When Stacy came back, they talked for a bit, then started to leave.

Chris, a basketball player, was first out the door. He was greeted by a bright light in his face and a rough voice, "Don't move or I'll blow your head off."

Terrified, Chris stopped. Was he about to be mugged and robbed? He was pulled roughly around and thrown against the wall. His arms were forced behind his back, and his fear grew.

Chris was almost relieved to hear the click of the handcuffs being snapped in place. At least he wasn't going to be killed. But why were the police there?

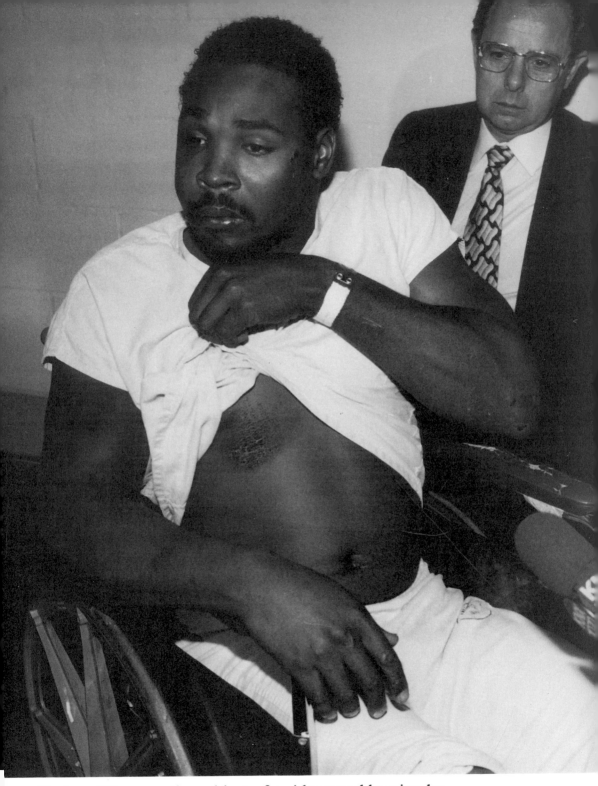

Rodney King was the subject of a videotaped beating by police officers of the Los Angeles Police Department. The officers were acquitted of charges of police brutality.

The officer took Chris to the patrol car parked at the curb. When Chris tried to ask what was going on, the officer rudely told him to shut up.

When Stacy came out, another officer came up to her. "Wait a minute," she said. "This is my house."

Just then, a neighbor hurried over and recognized Stacy. "I'm sorry," he said. "I didn't know who was in the house. I just knew it was empty and was worried when I saw lights come on."

The officers listened to the neighbor and Stacy. They agreed that there had been a mistake. One officer did apologize to Stacy.

Meanwhile, the officer who had treated Chris so roughly came over to release him. Chris figured he'd get an apology.

What he got was a threat. The officer told him he'd better watch out. Next time he wouldn't get off so easily.

Chris was stunned. He hadn't done anything wrong. Why was this officer treating him like scum?

An unfortunate reality that we face today is that teenagers are often hassled by police. African-American males are hassled more than any other group. This is a clear violation of the civil rights of a group of citizens.

In a study made by sociologists at the University of Florida in 1992, blacks or Hispanics were victims of 97 percent of the brutality cases reported; 93 percent of the officers involved were white. From 1990 to mid-1992, a survey of newspapers showed reports of 130 incidents of police brutality against minorities, contrasted with only two cases of brutality against whites.

Many of the problems between police officers and some groups are caused by prejudice and racism. One definition of *prejudice* is "an attitude based on prejudgment." We form an attitude about people without knowing them. Racism is a form of prejudice based on a person's racial heritage.

There is a long history of racism among certain members of the police force. In the 1950s and 1960s, police stopped and arrested members of minority groups far more often than whites. These problems continue to grow, and people on both sides are angry and defensive.

This book cannot deal with all the roots and causes of prejudice and racism. But there are things all of us can do to avoid confrontations with police.

The National Black Police Association offers the following suggestions:

- Never challenge or provoke the police. Remember, they are armed and you are not. *Never* run from the police.
- If you are stopped while driving, pull over and stay cool. Present your papers when asked. Don't make any sudden moves.
- If you are stopped on the street, stay calm. Identify yourself when asked, but don't

The police do have a right to question you. They do not have a right to harass you.

be uncooperative. Don't make any move that could be considered a threat.

- If the police try to enter your home, you do not have to let them in unless they have a warrant. If they don't have a warrant but insist on coming in, stay calm. Get their badge numbers, and tell them you don't consent to a search. Report the incident later.
- If you are arrested, demand that your parents be present. You can also demand an attorney, and you should not answer questions until you have talked to your parents and your attorney.

In most situations it's wise to keep in mind the words of one police officer, "The basic rule of most officers is, 'I will treat you exactly the way you treat me.' "

If you are ever unjustly stopped, the best response is to be calm and polite. Even if you don't think there is a reason to stop you, the officer might have one.

Suppose you are driving a beat-up old car in a nice neighborhood at night. The regular patrol officer will probably wonder why you are there. So you are pulled over.

The officer asks to see your driver's license. The next question is probably, "What are you doing here?"

Your first impulse may be to say it's none of the officer's business. You didn't do anything wrong. He had no business stopping you.

You may be right about not having done anything wrong, but you are wrong in thinking an officer can't stop you.

What An Officer Can Do

A police officer has two major responsibilities, to enforce the laws, and to maintain public order. Crime prevention is part of that second responsibility. Therefore, an officer *can* stop you if he or she suspects something is wrong.

Stopping and questioning a person is part of

a *field interrogation.* This is a legal police activity.

If an officer stops you on suspicion, he is going to be wary. Trying to evade his questions or refusing to answer will only make trouble for you. He also will object to your attitude.

You should just tell the officer politely why you are there. Maybe you were on your way to a movie and got lost. Whatever the reason, a polite explanation could end the situation.

But what happens if politeness doesn't work? What if you run into an officer like the one Chris did?

First of all, *don't try to settle the issue on the scene.* Answer the officer's questions. If he or she makes rude or insulting remarks, don't be sarcastic or nasty. Remember, anything an officer sees as a possible threat will make him or her move to the next step of force. Just take care of the business at hand.

A police liaison officer at a high school puts it this way: "It's just like when a teacher makes you do something that isn't fair. If you start sounding off in the classroom, it's just going to make the teacher mad and get you a detention. It's much smarter to keep your mouth shut. Do what you are told and then go talk to the principal or the dean about it."

In the case of police harassment, do the same thing. After the encounter is over, make a report.

How to Make a Report

First, you should get the officer's name and badge number at the scene. Officers are required to give that information when asked, but some may refuse to tell you. In that case, try to get the number of the patrol car. The number is usually printed in the decal on the side of the car.

Even if you can't get the information at the scene, it is still available to you. Call the station house and ask for Incident Information. Tell the person who answers the phone that you want information about an officer who just responded to a call. Each call is assigned an Incident Number, which is logged in the computer with the name of the officer who responded.

The operator will ask you why you want the information. Explain that you were involved in the incident and you were treated badly. You want to file a complaint against the officer.

You will then be put through to the Professional Standards Department. This department used to be called Internal Affairs, but it has changed in most police departments.

What happens next depends on the seriousness of the complaint. If the officer assaulted you, there will be a complete investigation. The officer could then be charged and put on trial. In less serious cases, the officer will receive a reprimand. In either case, the complaint becomes part of his or her file. Too many complaints can lead to a

If you are hassled by a police officer, you have every right to file a complaint with the police department.

temporary or permanent suspension from duty.

Under no circumstances should misconduct go unreported, and most good officers encourage reporting it. Officers who harass citizens make the job harder for all the others.

Chapter 4

Seeing It from the Other Side

"**A**s a law enforcement officer, my fundamental duty is to serve mankind: to safeguard lives and property, to protect the innocent against deception, the weak against oppression or intimidation, and the peaceful against violence . . .

". . . I will never act officiously or permit personal feelings, prejudices, animosities, or friendships to influence my decisions. With no compromise for crime and with relentless prosecution of criminals, I will enforce the law courteously and appropriately without fear or favor, malice or ill will, never employing unnecessary force or violence. . ."

This is part of the oath of office a person takes when he or she becomes a police officer. Most officers take that oath very seriously.

"Yeah, right," you may be thinking. "But what about those officers who hassled Greg and Chris?"

Police Officers of the New York City Police Academy, such as these recent graduates, take their oath of office seriously.

The sad truth is that some officers do ignore the code of ethics. They are the ones who make the headlines. They are also the ones who make it difficult for all the other officers to do their job.

Another sad truth is that we have become a very violent society. We can't sort out the good officers from the bad ones, and they can't tell the good guys from the bad guys.

Does that mean it's okay for some officers to harass people? No, it certainly doesn't. But nothing can change unless people on both sides of the issue learn to stop judging each other.

The relationship between police officers and certain groups is like two bullies on a playground: They draw a line in the dirt and yell at each other across it. They don't even think about going to the other side to find out what the other person is like.

Perhaps if we all stepped over that line a few times it would help.

Crossing the Line

Police officers should know the neighborhoods they patrol and the kids in the area.

Likewise, we should not blame all police officers for the behavior of some. We all remember the Los Angeles riots in 1992 after the acquittal of the police officers accused of beating Rodney King. Many people blamed the police and decided that all officers are bad.

The truth is, not all officers are bad, just as not all teenagers are bad. But we won't know that if we just listen to the news or popular opinion.

Maybe we should take the time to learn what a typical day is like to a patrol officer. During his shift he responds to a variety of calls.

His day might start at an accident site where an elderly man has been crushed in a car crash. The other driver, who was drunk, wasn't even hurt.

Then he may go to the home of an elderly

The 1992 Los Angeles riots are one example of what can happen when control over law and order is lost. In addition to the fighting, many buildings were set on fire, and hundreds of stores were looted.

woman who was beaten and robbed. Later, he has to arrest two teenage boys who robbed the woman for money to buy drugs.

He may be sent to a field where the body of a little girl was found. She had been abducted and strangled. The man who is eventually arrested turns out to be a repeat offender. He had been convicted of indecency with a minor but had served only a fraction of his sentence.

This is not offered as an excuse for an officer's behavior. Nobody should let the negative aspects of their job affect their treatment of people. But it illustrates the frustrations officers face.

Officers also have to deal with public attitudes that are often far from positive. Many people blame the police for the increase in crime. This builds a wall of resentment between the public and the police.

Chapter 5

Breaking Down the Walls

P olice departments are aware that changes need to be made. The attitudes and behavior that maintain a barrier between officers and the people have to be corrected. Many departments have programs to combat racism and prejudice. They also offer counseling and stress-management seminars to help officers handle the frustrations of their job more effectively. Some cities have Police Community Projects in which the police and citizens work together to fight crime.

A similar effort is the Community Police Program, in which officers walk beats and get to know the people. They work out of neighborhood mini-stations instead of large precincts.

In New Haven, Connecticut, arrests were down after one year of Community Policing. The murder rate and drive-by shootings decreased.

Other cities also noticed a decline in crime after

officers started patrolling on foot. More important, however, is how people come to feel in their neighborhoods. "Policemen are viewed as partners," says Mayor Sharpe James of Newark, New Jersey, "not members of an occupying force."

Things are also changing now that many officers are becoming better educated. Most departments require that recruits have at least two years of college; some departments require four years.

You may wonder what education has to do with the problems between police and people. It enables us to look at a situation with a broader view. We're not so quick to make snap judgments.

One social worker believes that education will make a big difference. "When more officers know how to control a situation through intellect," she says, "they won't have to rely on brute force."

What You Can Do

In bridging this gap between the police and the public, we need to take a few steps, too.

An excellent opportunity for young people to understand the police better is the Explorer Program. This program is affiliated with the Boy Scouts of America. If your city doesn't offer it, you could help get one started by contacting the Boy Scouts in your area.

Young people who are Explorers receive varied training. One aspect of the program is allowing

Many police departments are making an effort to get to know the people in their communities better.

young people to experience police work. They are trained in traffic accident investigations, firearms use and safety, crime prevention, and arrest and search techniques.

The Explorers spend time working with officers at the police station and out on patrol. Their assistance with routine police work is highly appreciated, and the young people enjoy getting to know the officers better.

Another way to broaden your knowledge is to ride patrol with officers. It is a good opportunity to see the job through their eyes and understand why they act the way they do. To ride patrol, simply make a request at the police station.

Another way officers and young people are breaking down barriers is through a school liaison officer. Students are encouraged to stop by the office and talk to the officer if they have problems. The liaison officer also acts as a mediator in potential fight situations.

What Needs to Be Done

In an article in *Ebony* magazine (July 1991), Hans J. Massaquoi wrote about the problem of harassment by police and public reactions to it. He encouraged people not to think of all police officers as mean and unprofessional. That only damages respect for all the officers who are dedicated public servants.

Massaquoi also offered suggestions to police departments to solve some of their problems:

- Set higher educational and psychological standards for recruiting officers.
- Improve psychological testing and background checks to screen out potentially volatile persons.
- Have frequent psychological tests for signs of burnout and other problems.
- Rotate officers between high-stress and low-stress assignments to avoid burnout.

Some people believe that setting higher educational requirements for police officers may help with the problems of police prejudice and harassment.

- Educate officers about the people and the culture of neighborhoods where they serve.
- Increase the number of police/community programs to reduce the "us/them" factor.
- Hire more black police officers and assign them to black communities.
- Break the "blue code" of police silence. Make officers who witness brutal acts by fellow officers equally responsible if they fail to stop the act and fail to report it.
- Make officers financially responsible if their actions result in costly lawsuits to the city.
- Replace police chiefs in departments that have a high incidence of police brutality.
- Have civilian review boards in which complaints receive a speedy hearing.
- Organize community action to force officials to deal with the problem of police brutality.

Chapter 6

Can I Be Searched?

*F*rancine walked through the metal detectors at the school's front door. They'd been there for a year now, so she was pretty used to them. She tried to make sure she had nothing in her purse to trigger the alarm. It was so embarrassing the day the alarm rang and everyone stared. It was also embarrassing to have the security guard go through her purse. She hated it.

No one likes to be searched. Our privacy is very important to us, especially when we haven't done anything wrong. It's also humiliating to have a stranger look through our things.

In the past, people were not searched so often. An increase in crime and terrorism in the past twenty years has increased the need for security. Police officers and security guards can now legally search people under certain circumstances:

Security checkpoint   If you go through a metal detector and trigger the alarm, your bags can be searched. The officer can run a hand-held detector around you. He or she can also ask you to empty your pockets.

This applies to checkpoints at schools, airports, some government buildings, and elsewhere.

Consequences   If you attempt to bring a weapon into a place where it is prohibited, you will be arrested.

Schools   School lockers can be searched at any time. They are legally the property of the school, so it is not an invasion of privacy.

Your bags or purse *cannot* be searched without "probable cause." Probable cause has to be more than a suspicion of something wrong. Triggering the alarm of a metal detector is probable cause. Having a drug-sniffing dog stop at your bag is probable cause.

Consequences   If drugs or weapons are found in your locker or in your bags, you can be arrested. The seriousness of the drug charge depends on the quantity and the type of drugs found. Possession of one marijuana cigarette is less serious than one ounce of cocaine.

Arrest   A search is legal at the time of arrest. Officers can search you, your belongings, and your car if you are driving. They *cannot* search you if they stop you on a traffic violation unless there is an outstanding warrant for your arrest.

Your school has the right to search your locker at any time.

Perhaps you forgot to take care of that speeding ticket six months ago. When you don't pay the fine and miss your court date, a warrant is issued. Since you ignored the law, you are in contempt of court, and that is serious.

But how does the officer know about that old speeding ticket? Every time an officer stops a car, he or she calls the station to "run" the license plate number. This is a computer check for outstanding warrants. Many criminals are arrested when officers stop them for routine violations.

A police officer *cannot* search you on suspicion. Let's return to the incident of driving your old car in a nice neighborhood. If an officer stops you just to find out why you are there, you can't be searched. But if there was a report of a car like yours leaving the scene of a crime, you could be searched. That gives the officer probable cause.

Consequences During an arrest on one charge, if the search turns up evidence of another crime, you can be charged for that, too.

Others You can be searched if an officer thinks you might have a weapon. At concerts, parades, or other large gatherings where officers provide safety, they can search people whom they suspect of having a gun.

They can also search if they have been called about a disturbance. Perhaps rival gangs have gathered at a street corner and start hassling each other. A homeowner sees the disturbance and is afraid a fight will break out, so he calls the police. For safety reasons, the police can search for weapons.

In most cases, the officer will only search your car and your belongings. If there is a strong suspicion that you have a weapon, you could be frisked; that is, searched by running hands over your body. You would also be frisked at the time of an arrest. A woman officer must be present when a female is frisked.

If you think you have been illegally searched, you can file a complaint. You should talk to an attorney first to make sure you are right. If the illegal search was part of an arrest, your attorney will act on it.

To know what is legal and what is not, you should know the laws in your state. One officer suggests reading the penal code of your state. "If you don't know the laws," he says, "how can you stay out of trouble?"

If you don't know the laws, you can't protect yourself, either.

What If I'm Arrested?

The Bill of Rights contains two amendments that deal with your legal rights at the time of arrest. The Fifth Amendment says that the accused "shall not be compelled to be a witness against himself." That means that you do not have to answer

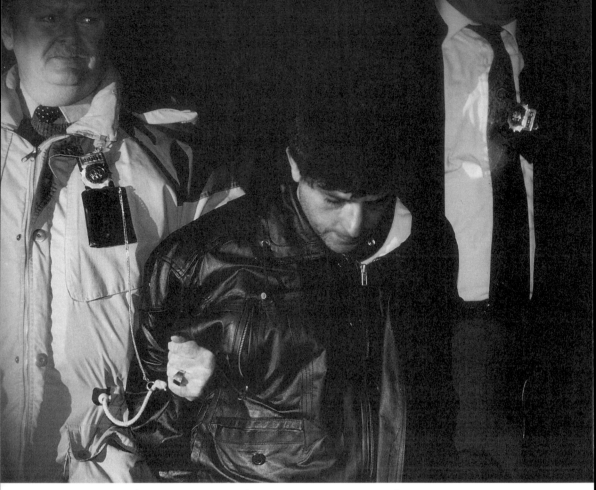

You have certain rights if you are arrested.

questions if your answers would show you to be guilty of a crime.

No one can force or bully you into answering questions. If a police officer uses force to frighten you into admitting a crime, that evidence cannot be used against you.

Your rights must be read to you at the time of arrest. Anyone who has watched cop shows on TV is familiar with the Miranda rights statement: "You have the right to remain silent. Anything you say can and will be used against you in a court of law.

You have the right to talk to an attorney and have him present with you while you are being questioned. If you cannot afford to hire an attorney one will be appointed to represent you."

The officers must ask you if you understand those rights. Then you will be asked if you wish to answer questions. In most cases it is not a good idca to talk without the advice of a lawyer.

Most of us are unaware of the details of law. That's why the Sixth Amendment gives us the right to "have the assistance of counsel for defense." This assistance must begin the moment you are arrested. It doesn't matter whether or not you committed the crime.

Chapter 7
Dial 911

*T*ommy wasn't sure, but he thought those kids were trying to break into the house across the street. Keeping to the shadows of the trees, Tommy edged closer to see better.

Sure enough, the kids had screwdrivers and were trying to get the screen off the window.

At first, Tommy wasn't sure what to do. Should he try to make them stop? No. He was too scared to do that. He should call somebody.

Tommy turned and ran home. Once inside, he dialed 911.

If you ever see a crime in progress, report it. You should also report anything you suspect might be a crime or leading to one.

People who pay attention to what is going on and report suspicious things help officers a great deal. They also help to keep crime down.

The best thing you can do if you see a crime being committed is to call the police or dial 911.

Never enter a house that looks as though it has been broken into.

Neighborhoods with active Crime Watch groups have less crime than those without such groups. So reporting crime helps keep you safe.

When Do You Dial 911?

For serious crimes such as murder, rape, or robbery, you dial 911. You should also use it to report a "crime in progress" or a situation of extreme danger. If you saw a bunch of kids starting a fire in a park, you would definitely dial 911.

In most cities, dialing 911 puts you through to a dispatcher who handles both the police department and the fire department. Tell the dispatcher what you saw and give as much information as possible. Describe the person, and try to give details: The person had tan boots and a blue baseball cap worn backward.

The dispatcher will let you know if the officer will want you as a witness. You need not be a witness if you don't want to be. In a nonviolent crime, the officer probably won't even contact you. In other crimes, the officer will check out the crime scene, then take a statement from you.

If you should ever be on the scene of a drive-by shooting, the first thing to do is protect yourself. Drop to the ground or get behind something that will shield you. Make sure the threat is over before you move. Then go to the nearest phone and dial 911.

The information the dispatcher will want is location, time, description of vehicle, number of persons in car, license number if possible, and type of weapon if possible.

To be safe, you should never go back to the scene of a violent crime. Stay in the house and wait for an officer to come to you to take your statement.

When Do You Not Dial 911?

To report nonthreatening crimes, dial the regular number for the police department. Dial that number also to call to report crimes "not in progress." A crime not in progress might be theft.

Another might be an assault that is already over. Two guys beat you up, but they've already run away. You want to report it, but you are no longer in immediate danger. You would not dial 911.

If you are in doubt, use 911. If you come home from school and find your back door broken open, you don't know whether a burglar is still inside. Since there is a strong possibility of danger, report it by using 911.

Don't Abuse the System

In most states it is a Class B misdemeanor to dial 911 and give a false report. It is also a crime to make a "silent call": to dial 911 and not speak.

It is easy to see why false reports are a crime. Too often officers are unable to respond to a real emergency because the dispatcher was tied up with a false report. In fact, an officer in New York City was killed in 1993 while responding to a false 911 report.

Don't do it. It's never funny. And the calls can and will be traced.

Chapter 8

Tips on Confrontations

It starts out with a small group of friends getting together on a Friday night. Tammy's parents are out of town, and they are just going to have a little party. But word gets around school, and about 40 people crash the party. Cars with stereos blasting are parked up and down the street, and someone calls the police.

The first thing the officers do is control the situation outside. They give people a chance to get in their cars and leave. If they don't get cooperation, arrests may be made, especially if there are signs of drinking or drugs.

Facing such a large group, the officers are bound to be a little tense. They don't know how the people may act, and they are prepared for the worst. If the situation starts to get out of hand, they react with force. They are trained to take whatever steps are necessary to control a crowd.

If it's your party, the police will then come to your door. You don't have to let them in. But if you haven't been drinking and have nothing to hide, it is in your best interest to let them come in.

But He Started It

You're leaving the gym after basketball practice and the guy who's been after you all week jumps you. You've had enough of his pushing you around, and you fight back.

Before you know it, someone has called the police. What should you do?

First of all, settle yourself down. If the officer thinks you are still a threat, he or she will treat you harshly.

If both people involved in the fight cooperate, the officer will tell you to go your ways and learn to settle your differences without fighting.

If you refuse to leave or become belligerent, the officer may arrest you for disorderly conduct. That is a Class C misdemeanor.

In situations involving numbers of kids fighting, the police use more force to get control. The possibility of arrests is also greater.

A police officer explains, "We will round up everybody that's there. Then we'll try to find out what started the fight. If there are no weapons involved and it looks like typical kid stuff, we'll just tell them all to go home.

No matter who started a fight, all participants are responsible for their actions.

"Arrests will be made only if the kids don't cooperate. Although there could be an arrest made later if one kid decides to file a complaint against another kid for assault."

If you are ever involved in such a situation, don't try to run away. The officers need to talk to everyone there. Stay calm and obey the officer even if you don't agree.

Keep Your Distance

Police officers on the job never stand close to people. They don't like people to stand close to them, either, for a very good reason: They don't want someone to grab their weapon. Officers are killed every year with their own weapon.

You should never touch an officer on duty, even to get his attention. Any movement toward him may be seen as a threat.

If you want to ask an officer for directions, walk around in front of him and ask your question.

Conclusion

People often forget that a police officer's job is to help people. The Rodney King incident, among others, has raised public awareness of police brutality. But you should also remember that police are generally the good guys.

Glossary

assault Physical attack.

blue code Code of loyalty among police officers that makes them protect each other.

Bureau of Alcohol, Tobacco, and Firearms Federal agency responsible for enforcing laws concerning firearms, tobacco, and alcohol.

community service Alternative to jail time or a fine, in which offenders work in programs that help people.

Customs Service Federal agency authorized to collect taxes on imported goods and to investigate cases of smuggling.

disorderly conduct Fighting in public, disturbing the peace, or other petty offense.

dispatcher Person who answers calls to police and fire departments and sends help.

Drug Enforcement Agency Federal agency responsible for enforcing drug laws.

felony Serious crime such as murder, burglary, rape, robbery.

Federal Bureau of Investigation Agency responsible for investigating violations of federal law.

harassment Repeated verbal or physical attacks.

Immigration Border Patrol Federal agency that controls the movement of illegal aliens across the borders of the United States.

misdemeanor Less serious crime than a felony, such as a traffic violation, simple assault, truancy, vagrancy, or disorderly conduct.

municipal court City court that handles nonfelony cases.

penal code Book of the laws of the state.

police brutality Excessive force used by the police in dealing with a situation or person.

Postal Inspection Service Department of the Postal Service that deals with crimes committed through the mail: fraud, pornography, and others.

Secret Service Agency Federal Agency that provides protection to the President, other leading public figures, and their families.

warrant Legal document signed by a judge permitting police to make a search or an arrest.

Help List

NATIONAL BLACK POLICE ASSOCIATION
3251 Mt. Pleasant Street NW
Washington, DC 20010-2103

Founded in 1972 to improve relations between police officers and black neighborhoods. Publishes a newsletter that reports on laws, court decisions, and general police actions.

NATIONAL POLICE OFFICERS ASSOCIATION
  OF AMERICA
P.O. BOX 22129
Louisville, KY 40252-0129

Founded in 1955, this organization conducts educational programs. It publishes a magazine, *National Police Review.*

NATIONAL UNITED LAW ENFORCEMENT
  OFFICERS ASSOCIATION
256 East McLemore Avenue
Memphis TN 38106

Founded in 1969, the association develops community-based programs to improve relations between officers and communities. Offers telecommunications service: Search for Answers (information hot line) 1-800-533-4649. Publishes quarterly newsletter: *National United Law Enforcement Officers Association Student Chapter News*.

POLICE FOUNDATION
1001 22nd Street NW
Washington, DC 20037

Founded in 1970 to increase police effectiveness in controlling crime. Publishes books, reports, and handbooks.

In Canada
Policing Services Division
Police Support Programs Branch
(416) 965-6071

For Further Reading

Adams, Thomas F. *Law Enforcement: An Introduction to the Police Role in the Community*. Englewood Cliffs: Prentice-Hall, 1968.

Arnold, Caroline. *Who Keeps Us Safe?* New York: Franklin Watts, 1982.

Baker, Mark. *Cops: Their Lives in Their Own Words*. New York: Simon & Schuster, 1985.

Bayley, David H., and Mendelsohn, Harold. *Minorities and the Police: Confrontation in America*. New York: Free Press, 1969.

Broekel, Ray. *Police*. Chicago: Children's Press, 1981.

Brown, David. *Someone Always Needs a Policeman*. New York: Simon & Schuster, 1972.

Cooper, Jason. *Police Stations*. Vero Beach, FL: Rourke, 1992.

Delattre, Edwin J. *Character and Cops: Ethics in Policing*. Washington, DC: American

Enterprise Institute for Public Policy
Research, 1989.

Dolan, Edward F., and Scariano, Margaret M. *The
Police in American Society*. New York:
Franklin Watts, 1988.

Hewett, Joan. *Motorcycle on Patrol: The Story of a
Highway Officer*. New York: Clarion Books,
1986.

Robinson, Barry. *On the Beat: Policemen at Work*.
New York: Harcourt, Brace & World, 1968.

Seagraves, Roy W. *Juveniles Have Rights, Too*.
Belmont, CA: Fearon/Janus, 1987.

Sparrow, Malcolm K. *Beyond 911: A New Era for
Policing*. New York: Basic Books, 1990.

Trojanowicz, Robert C. *Community Policing: A
Contemporary Perspective*. Cincinnati:
Anderson Pub. Co., 1990.

Index

About the Author
Maryann Miller has been published in numerous maga-
zines and Dallas newspapers. She has served as editor,
columnist, reviewer, and feature writer.
    Married for over thirty years, Ms. Miller is the mother
of five children. She and her husband live in Omaha,
Nebraska.

Photo Credits
Cover, pp. 29, 50, 55 by Lauren Piperno; pp. 2, 9, 11, 22, 25,
31, 37, 46, 57 © AP/Wide World Photos; pp. 7, 16, 18, 39,
43, 49 by Kim Sonsky